INDEX

Published by New Generation Publishing in 2015

First Edition

www.newgeneration-publishing.com

New Generation Publishing

Dedicated

To

The Child

in

All of us

BURPED (AGED 1)

Now here I am a baby, lying on my back
The pillow is all fluffy, and the mattress it is flat.
I have a brand new dummy and a noisy rattle too
And two soft and cuddly rabbits, one is pink and one is blue.

When I look up there is no sky, just a nice blue ceiling
And a musical bird that turns around, oh it is so very pleasing.
I can't walk yet but I can crawl, but it hurts my knees a lot
I hope it doesn't rub my skin off, because I haven't got a lot.

I had a really full up tum, mummy burped me on her shoulder
I see the window is now open, and my bottom feels much colder.
Now I'm lying down and all is still, but the pretty birds still flying
Perhaps I'll go to sleep right now; at least I will keep on trying

SISTERS (AGED 2)

I have got a little sister; they all fuss her yes they do
But she is only nine months old, and I am just past two.
Now she has got a funny name, honest it is true
They pick her up and with a smile, say oochey coochey coo.

Its oochey coocheys birthday soon and she'll be one already
My mummy brought a big brown thing, I think that it's called teddy.
But I have got a bright blue ball, and a shiny thing called trumpet
When I get cross I pick it up, and then I start to thump it.

I'm tired now all covered up, a belly full of milk
A lovely stitched up keep warm thing, my grandma made from silk.
And little coochey is sleeping, sucking on her thumb
Another day for brother and sister finally is done.

AUNTIES (AGED 3)

I have a strange old auntie, my mummy calls her flo
She hasn't got a lot of hair, but her fingernails still grow.
She covers me in kisses, and calls me by my name
Then pinches me upon the cheek, she's always been the same.

When we sit down to dinner, she always clears her plate
Because we have steak and kidney, and auntie thinks it's great.
But on a day called Sunday, I didn't know what to do
Her really shiny teeth came loose, and fell into the stew.

Now auntie flo is leaving, she has someone to meet
She says he is a pensioner, who lives just down the street.
"I'll see you all next Sunday, hope you're in when I arrive"
Well auntie flo is eighty two, so what happens when you're five?

PLAY SCHOOL (AGED 4)

I am sitting on a wooden chair, in a great big place
And I have lots of shiny tears, running down my face.
My mummy has gone with a kiss goodbye; she said I have to stay
And now a horrible little kid is asking me to play.

What do I do, don't like it here, there's paint all down my thumb
There's a lady who is smiling, but I'm not having fun.
She offered me some jelly; it was wobbling on my plate
My mummy is coming back at three, I hope she isn't late.

Well it's nearly time to go now, I don't know if I'm glad
I cannot wait to tell my mummy, about the fun I've had.
I played in sand, had jelly, painted a banana red
I won't stay home tomorrow; I will come back here instead

SEASIDE (AGED 5)

I'm here at a place called seaside, with a big hat on my head
The back of my hands are burning, and my little face is red.
I've just had an ice cream cone, and a sandwich from the car
I wanted to paddle in the sea, but mummy said, don't go far.

Now I have sand between my toes, and seaweed on my bonnet
I want to pick a rock up, but it's got sharp bits all on it.
I held a shell up to my ear, but I couldn't hear the sea
It was then a saw a great big seagull, staring down at me.

Well the day is nearly over, soon we will go home
Daddy is pulling funny faces, while mummy is on the phone
Me I am in the back seat, trying to have a rest
Spent a lovely day at the seaside, it's been the very best.

EASTER (AGED 6)

I had a funny egg at breakfast, it wasn't from a chicken
It was chocolate wrapped in silver paper, and it had a creamy filling.
I asked my mum, said is it mine, and what kind of bird had laid it
She said it was from her and dad, and that a factory had made it.

I smiled a factory egg said I, a big bird or was it small
And when they are sitting on the nest, why don't they melt them all.
Oh don't be silly it's not a bird, it's a machine of metal and plastic
And lots of wheels all in a row, they really look fantastic.

Mum a factory is not an animal, not a bird not rabbit or fish
It's usually where you make something, like pretty patterns on a dish.
Then can you tell me mother please, or do I have to beg
Why the factory is not a bird, and yet it lays an egg.

?
EGGS
THISWAY
Jam

GHOSTS (AGED 7)

Wind against the window, rattle of the glass
My head beneath the covers will they just slip past.
Creeping ever creeping, to the corner of my bed
I can hear them laughing, little ghosts inside my head.

Soon they gather close to me; some are thin and short some tall
They just don't seem too bothered, by the light out in the hall.
Reaching ever reaching, for the covers of my bed
But ghosts are only pictures that live inside my head.

Shut my eyes quite tightly, how quietly I breathe
In the land of dreams soon, then they will all soon leave
Silent now my bedroom, light no longer on
Just a slight breeze blowing, now the ghosts have gone.

Ghosts

FRIENDS (AGED 8)

My friend who is my best friend has a short name he's called Sam
He says I am not his friend at all, but I know I really am.
I got him out of trouble when he lost his good friends ball
I said my friend's friend kicked it, and it went over the wall.

Some friends are friendly but then again, I think that some are not
But Jim, who is as old as me, is the best friend that I've got.
His friend is also my friend, we sometimes call him Bill
And he lives right next to his friend, at the bottom of the hill.

So who are friends and what are friends, but now I see it clearly
A Friend is a friend who has a friend; I think that's it well nearly.
So get a friend and keep a friend, and never lose them ever
For to keep a friend right to the end, well that takes someone clever

8

CHRISTMAS TIME (AGED 9)

I had to write this letter, to Santa Claus you see
To ask him if I am very good, what gift to leave for me.
I thought about a rocket, and then I thought about a train
Then thought about some soldiers, but I'll have a think again.

Now Christmas is a funny time, my gran gets drunk on sherry
We have a tree up with some lights, and holly with some berries.
We also have a turkey, and some roast potatoes to
My tooth is very loose right now; I don't know what to do.

But its bedtime now I'm sleepy, and it's snowing fast outside
But Santa's got his Rudolph, with his red nose for a guide.
My big old stockings hanging, empty on my bed
Shall I wait up for Santa, no I'll go to sleep instead?

Dear Santa
Santa C

DENTISTS (AGED 10)

Please sit down it won't take long; I wonder where my mother's gone
This chair although it's soft and warm, I notice that an arm is torn.
Please don't shine a light on me; I am very scared why can't see
By grinning in the way you do, I see your teeth are shiny too.

What's that thing that one there, the one that's fastened on the chair
It makes a noise just like a bee, it getting very close to me.
I'm sitting here no I won't move, I'll hold my breath as if to prove
That I can keep my mouth shut tight, what open up? oh well I might.

So don't forget when sucking on, crunchy sweets that fizz on tongue
Eating ice cream and chewing gum, when only thinking of your tum
For round the corner of this road, teeth disappear at ten years old
For Girls and boys who don't care, all end up in the dentist's chair.

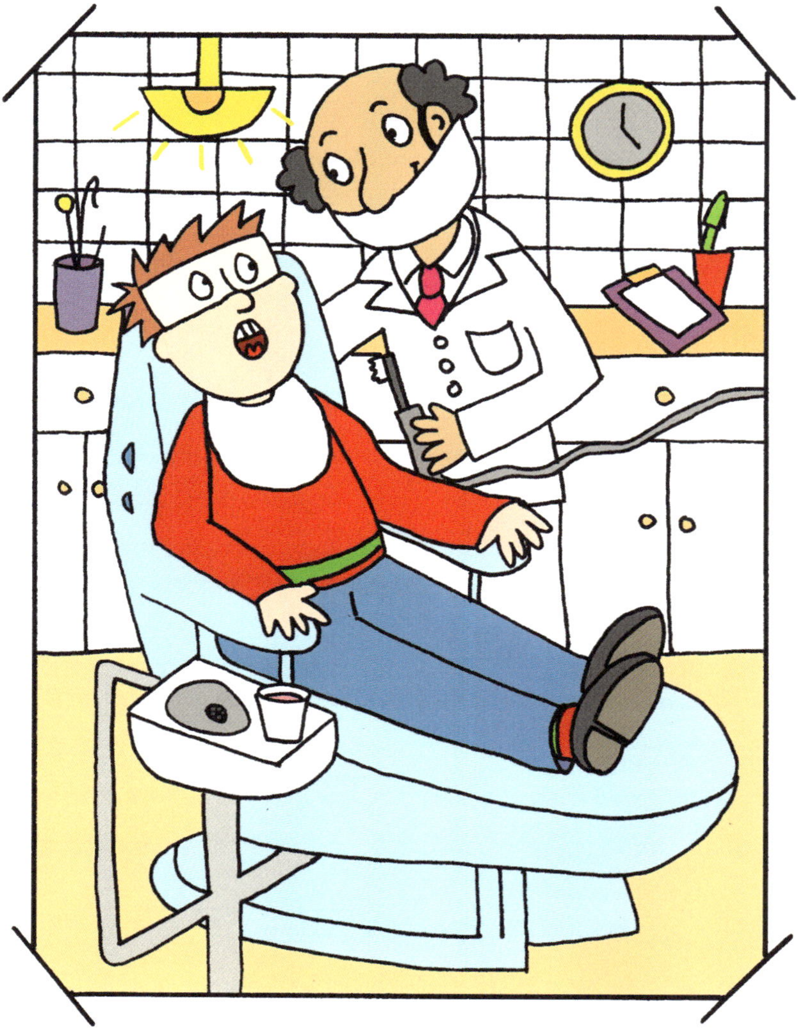

BROTHERS (AGED 11)

He's horrible my brother, he took my best school tie
And if that wasn't bad enough, he told our mum a lie.
He said that I had used it, for a lead to walk the dog
But I found it in his cardboard box, a bed for his pet frog.

Now last week it was Wednesday, he let my rabbit out
The poor thing hopped across the lawn, he chased it all about.
He put a fly that he had caught, in mums new sugar bowl
Then he lost my favourite marble, down a very deep dark hole.

So some brothers they are trouble, what do we have them for
Now he's taken my paper plane, and thrown it through the door.
But that's all right I heard mum, say he's got to have a filling
Someone said when he's in the chair; they will have to put the drill in.

RELIGION (AGED 12)

Someone told me gods a man, who lives up in the sky
It seems a very long way up, it is so very high.
Does he need special glasses, to see us far below
And when on bended knee we pray, does he really know

Now Sunday morning in the church, I sing a hymn or two.
I am not very good with high notes, but what else can I do.
The cross upon the alters small, the vicar is dressed in white
Could he be a doctor, when he goes home at night?

A funny word religion, all those prayers and songs and God
I wonder if people think of it, when eating chips with cod.
But turn the cheek and please be good, that doesn't sound so bad
I must try and remember that, when I upset my dad.

Lightning Source UK Ltd.
Milton Keynes UK
UKIC01n0323250216
269030UK00010B/58